EL SALVADOR

Wager for peace

GW00601082

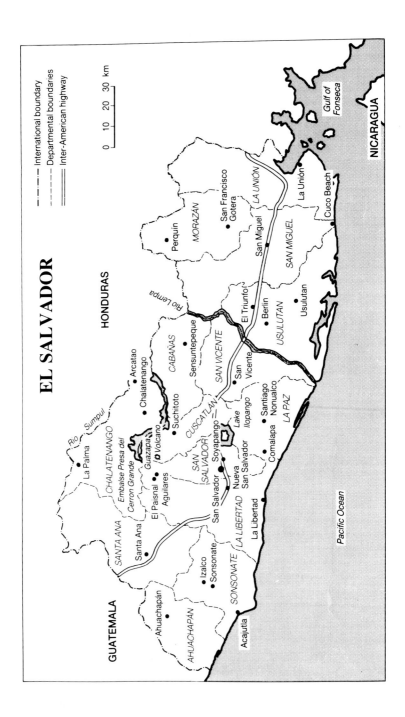

Contents

Wager for peace

Introduction

The signing of Peace Accords by the government of El Salvador and the Farabundo Martí National Liberation Front (FMLN) on 16 January 1992 produced unprecedented rejoicing in the country. Over 100,000 people took part in the celebrations in the capital San Salvador, thousands with FMLN banners and placards, entertained by formerly banned pop groups, and the whole scene covered live by the formerly clandestine radio stations, Venceremos and Farabundo Martí. Smaller celebrations took place all over the country. These scenes were repeated on 1 February as the ceasefire came into effect and the leaders and fighters of the FMLN moved about openly in the capital for the first time since the outbreak of the war in 1980.

The jubilation was understandable: the Accords, the result of nearly two years of tortuous negotiations under United Nations mediation, offered the possibility of ending 12 years of civil war and repression which had made this small Central American country a focus of international attention. Over 75,000 had lost their lives during the war, most of them civilians killed by the security forces and their related death squads.

The celebrations were above all an expression of relief. Previous talks in the 1980s had repeatedly raised and dashed hopes of peace, and though it was clear that the implementation of the Accords would prove as difficult and fraught with dangers as the negotiations themselves had been, Salvadoreans dared to hope that the movement towards peace and the construction of a new and more just society was now irreversible.

This *Comment* examines the negotiations against their background in the end of the Cold War, analyses the Peace Accords and chronicles the first 18 months of their implementation. It then looks at the challenges of reconciliation and reconstruction as the Accords affect various sectors of Salvadorean society, and argues that the international community continues to have a vital role both in the run-up to the 1994 elections and beyond.

Inequality and the causes of war

El Salvador is the most densely populated country in Latin America: in a land area of 8,000 square miles it has a population of over 5 million, with over 1 million living in the Greater San Salvador area. Over half the population is unable to meet basic food and medical needs. The country has the highest level of infant mortality in Central America. Forty-seven per cent of children suffer from malnutrition. According to the UN, illiteracy stood at 27 per cent in 1990 but was considered by some observers to be much higher.

Widespread poverty and the concentration of wealth in the hands of a small landowning elite were the underlying causes of the war, but the trigger was the persistent refusal of the elite to tolerate peaceful pressure for change. Fraudulent elections in 1972 and 1977 convinced many that only armed struggle could achieve the necessary political and social change, break the repressive control of the armed forces, and open the way for the rule of law to replace the corrupt and cowed judicial system.

As a rightwards-moving Christian Democrat Party (PDC) moved into government with the military in 1980, political forces on the left and the extreme right were growing and polarising. Increasing repression fuelled support for the emerging guerrilla movements which were soon to unite in the FMLN. Progressive Christian Democrats joined Social Democrats in the Revolutionary Democratic Front (FDR), a political alliance supporting the FMLN, while the ex-army major widely believed to be the founder of the death squads, Roberto D'Aubuisson, formed the Nationalist Republican Alliance party (ARENA), supported by hardliners in the military and financed by the most anti-reform sectors of the economic elite.

In 1981 the US administration under Ronald Reagan unveiled its doctrine of rolling back communism worldwide. El Salvador, where the FMLN had launched an offensive to greet the new administration, was seen as an urgent starting point. The insurgency was perceived by the United States as the next step of 'Soviet-Cuban expansion' into its 'backyard' after the 1979 Sandinista revolution in neighouring Nicaragua. Its strategists calculated that, with determined US backing, the Salvadorean army would make short work of the FMLN. Over the next 12 years the US government financed, trained and, to a degree, directed the activities of the Salvadorean military.

For the Salvadorean economy, like most economies in the Third World, the 1980s were a lost decade. With ever more unfavourable terms of trade, an increasing debt burden, and the costs of the war, the country became almost totally dependent on US aid (which amounted to US$6 billion over the decade). It has been estimated that FMLN sabotage alone cost over US$2 billion, and by 1988 almost 45 per cent of current government spending was going on defence and security. By the end of the 1980s important sectors of business were convinced that peace was an urgent economic necessity.

Pressures for peace

In 1983 the Contadora Group — Mexico, Venezuela, Colombia and Panama — was formed to seek a peaceful solution to Central America's tensions. Years of patient diplomacy bore no fruit, however, largely owing to the determination of the United States to remove the Sandinista government from power in Nicaragua. US hostility also sought to frustrate the demilitarisation proposals of the Esquipulas II process, named after the Guatemalan town where a regional peace agreement was signed in August 1987 by five Central American presidents.

For most of the 1980s, the United States remained wedded to a twin-pronged strategy of providing massive military aid to the Salvadorean military in pursuit of victory over the FMLN, while at the same time supporting the holding of elections to give the impression of 'democratic' normality.

Talks between Christian Democrat President José Napoleón Duarte and the FMLN in October 1987 ended without agreement because of the opposition of the Salvadorean armed forces and the US administration to any agreement short of an FMLN surrender and participation in elections on the government's terms. It was not until September 1989 that talks were resumed with Duarte's successor, President Alfredo Cristiani of ARENA, but they were brought to an abrupt end by a bomb attack on the headquarters of the FENASTRAS trade union federation on 31 October and the subsequent FMLN offensive of 11 November.

The series of talks, lasting almost two years, which ultimately produced the Peace Accords, was partly the result of profound changes in the international situation. The collapse of the Soviet Union undermined the Reagan-Bush crusade to defeat communism worldwide and to back the repression of popular movements in Central America on the grounds of the 'Soviet threat'. The deep economic crisis in the United States, caused in part by the policy of outbidding the Soviets in military spending, made the vast sums needed for widespread foreign involvements increasingly unrealistic and unpopular with an inward-looking Congress.

In El Salvador, the durability of the FMLN's military strength, demonstrated by the rebel offensive in November 1989, the biggest of the war, was the final proof that US policy had failed. Washington was forced to recognise that the Salvadorean army was incapable of defeating the FMLN without further aid on a scale unsustainable politically or economically. It decided to put pressure on President Cristiani to reach an agreement with the FMLN, overcoming resistance by the oligarchy and the armed forces.

For the FMLN too, the collapse of the Soviet Union and the East European communist regimes changed the world, undermining visions of revolutionary transformation and depriving them of potential allies. Nearer home the electoral defeat of the Sandinistas in Nicaragua in February 1990, following the US-sponsored counter-revolutionary war, showed that in the US 'backyard' movements for social change could not escape the continuing dominance of the United States.

Within El Salvador the war had reached stalemate, the death and destruction had produced war weariness on both sides, increasing the political cost of the struggle to both the government and FMLN.

Indeed, while the offensive launched by the FMLN on 11 November 1989 enabled the rebels to penetrate upper-class districts of the capital, thus destroying all pretence of political normality, the FMLN nevertheless failed to inflict a conclusive defeat on the army.

On the other hand, the decision of the military to retaliate with an act of wanton savagery removed the last shreds of the government's claim to be defending order and democracy. At a meeting of the army high command on 15 November attention focused on the Central American University (UCA), which the vice-minister of defence, Colonel Juan Orlando Zepeda, had publicly denounced as an FMLN centre of operations. Orders were given to kill Father Ignacio Ellacuría, the rector of the UCA, whom the army regarded as the leader of the 'subversives', and to leave no witnesses. The result was the murder on 16 November of six Jesuit priests and two women workers.

The international impact of this atrocity was a decisive factor in changing US policy towards El Salvador.

The UN and the emergence of the Accords

From April 1990, at the request of both sides, the UN acted as the mediator in a new series of negotiations, in the person either of the secretary-general, then Javier Pérez de Cuéllar, or of his representative, Alvaro de Soto. Both in the negotiation of the Accords and in their implementation, the UN played a vital role.

At a meeting in Caracas, Venezuela, in May 1990, the Salvadorean armed forces were for the first time represented and the ground rules for the negotiations proper were finally agreed. Negotiations took place over the next 15 months at meetings in Costa Rica, Venezuela and Mexico, but ground to a halt. The deadlock was broken only when the UN secretary-general invited both sides to meet him at the UN headquarters in New York on 16-17 September 1991. The most important of the meetings to date, it resulted in the signing of the New York Agreement (New York I) on 25 September. In this crucial agreement the FMLN finally abandoned its demand for the total disbanding of the army or the fusion of the army and FMLN forces.

The final stage of the negotiations began on 12 October in Mexico City and was pushed to a conclusion by Pérez de Cuéllar in New York on the last day of his mandate, 31 December 1991. A few minutes before midnight on 31 December 1991 a six-paragraph Act was signed, known as New York II, ending the 12-year civil war in El Salvador and setting 1 February 1992 as the formal beginning of the ceasefire.

Discussions continued in New York from 6 January until 14 January 1992, on which date agreement was reached on a calendar of implementation according to which the demobilisation of the FMLN and its integration into civilian life would be carried out within nine months of the ceasefire, in other words by 31 October.

The formal signing of the Peace Accords took place in a historic ceremony in Chapultepec Castle, Mexico City, soon after noon on 16 January, in the presence of the new UN secretary-general, Dr Boutros Boutros-Ghali, representatives of the FMLN, President Cristiani, the presidents of Mexico, Colombia and Venezuela and the Prime Minister of Spain (representing the four states known as the 'friends of the secretary-general'), other heads of state, US Secretary of State James Baker, a representative of the European Community and many other political and diplomatic figures.

Provisions of the Accords

The Accords signed by the Salvadorean government and the FMLN in Mexico in January 1992 covered all the agreements made by the two parties in the negotiations since April 1990. They provided for the demobilisation of the FMLN forces, the reduction and restructuring of the national army and the creation of a new civilian police force. The administration of justice and the electoral system were to be reformed, and a new office of human rights ombudsman established. A Truth Commission was to be established to investigate and publish the truth about the worst human rights abuses. The Accords included provisions for land redistribution and reconstruction in the areas most affected by the war and outlined principles for El Salvador's future economic development.

To supervise the process a Commission for the Consolidation of Peace (COPAZ) was to be set up, representing all the main Salvadorean political groups. The UN was to monitor the process through an observer mission, ONUSAL. A timetable was agreed for military demobilisation, starting with the declaration of a ceasefire on 1 February and ending on 31 October 1992.

The FMLN

The FMLN was required to concentrate its forces in 15 centres throughout the country, to stockpile its weapons and produce an inventory and then destroy them. Its forces were to be demobilised in five stages, and ex-combatants reintegrated into civilian life, with grants of land and financial assistance. The FMLN would subsequently be recognised as a political party.

The national army

The army was required to withdraw to barracks. By the end of November the five US-trained elite battalions, Belloso, Atonal, Atlacatl, Bracamonte and Arce, were to be disbanded, as were the paramilitary forces of the Civil Defence and Territorial Patrols, and over a period of two years the armed forces were to be reduced by half to around 30,000.

In a radical restructuring, the armed forces were to lose responsibility for public security, and the three security forces under army control, the National Guard, the Treasury Police and the National Police, were to be disbanded. The Salvadorean Legislative Assembly was given responsibility for supervising the military, and a new

7

training system was to be designed, including human rights education 'to stimulate a more harmonious relationship with civil society'.

The widely mistrusted National Intelligence Directorate was to be dissolved and replaced by a security service reporting to the president. The reforms also foresaw an end to the all-pervasive role of the army's press office, COPREFA, which during the war was key in forming public opinion through both its relations with the national press and its own regular television spot.

An Ad Hoc Commission, composed of three Salvadoreans with proven democratic credentials, was to be set up to examine the human rights records of all military officers and determine their suitability for service in the post-war period.

The police

Responsibility for public security was to pass to a new force, the National Civil Police, separate from the army and under the control of a civilian minister. The new police force would replace the previous security forces (the National Police, Treasury Police and National Guard), which had been under the control of the armed forces and had been held responsible by human rights groups for widespread abuses. It was envisaged that the majority of the recruits for the new police force would not have taken part directly in the armed conflict and the rest would come in equal numbers from former members of the old National Police and the FMLN. A new police academy was to be set up with a new training programme.

The judiciary and human rights

In an attempt to eliminate the politicisation of the Supreme Court, give it greater independence from government and, at the same time, reduce its absolute control over lower courts, various reforms were proposed. In future a two-thirds majority of the Legislative Assembly would be required for the election of Supreme Court judges instead of the previous simple majority, in order to reduce the possibility of the Court being packed with nominees of one party. Length of service was to be increased to nine years to provide greater stability. The Legislative Assembly would choose from a list of candidates submitted by the National Judicial Council, and this body also was in future to be elected by a two-thirds majority of deputies, as a precaution against political bias. The Council was also to be responsible for running the new Judicial Training School which was intended to raise the level of professionalism at all levels of the judiciary. The Accords stipulated that the judicial system was to receive 6 per cent of government spending in order to eliminate the need for traditionally poorly paid judges to earn extra income as lawyers or notaries. This budget increase was also intended to reduce the temptation to accept bribes.

An innovation was the creation of the new post of human rights ombudsman, with the task of monitoring and promoting respect for human rights and investigating specific cases and complaints.

The electoral system

In an effort to eliminate bias in the electoral system, the Accords provided that all political parties would take part in the drawing up and updating of the electoral register. The upheavals of the war make this an extremely complex task. Hundreds of thousands of people are not registered, particularly returnees and the populations of former FMLN-controlled zones. Many of these people do not possess the necessary documents for registration; in many cases they were lost when villages were bombed or deserted. Finally, only some 6,000 of those who have died over the past eight years have been removed from the register.

The other main electoral reform was the creation of a Supreme Electoral Tribunal, to be elected by a two-thirds majority of the Legislative Assembly, to ensure broad political support.

The Truth Commission

Modelled on a similar body set up in Chile after the end of the Pinochet dictatorship in 1990, a Truth Commission, composed of three distinguished non-Salvadoreans, was to have the task of uncovering the truth about the worst human rights abuses since 1980 by all sides, studying the impunity with which the Salvadorean military and security forces committed abuses, making legal, political, or administrative recommendations to prevent a repetition of such abuses, and to promote reconciliation. It was thus on the one hand an attempt to compensate for the past inadequacies of the Salvadorean police and judicial system, and on the other to create the basis for a new society by revealing the mechanisms of human rights abuses and proposing safeguards for the future. Questions of trial and punishment were not within the commission's brief.

Economic and social policy

The Accords called for the completion of the existing agrarian reform law, passed by the Christian Democrat administration in the early 1980s, by distributing properties over 245 hectares and the lands already owned by the state. The government agreed to recognise current tenure of land in the conflict zones, to purchase these properties from the legal owners and resell to those who now occupied them on the same subsidised terms as under the agrarian reform programme. The land distribution was intended to benefit primarily the ex-combatants of the two armies. A National Reconstruction Plan (PNR) was to be drawn up for the reconstruction and development of the conflict zones with the support of the United Nations Development Programme (UNDP). Longer-term consultation and discussion over economic policy was to be take place in a new body, the Forum for Economic and Social Consensus (FES), composed of representatives of government, business and labour in equal numbers.

COPAZ

COPAZ was defined in the Accords as 'a mechanism for the monitoring of, and the participation of civilian society in, the process of the changes resulting from the negotiations, in relation both to the armed forces, in particular, and to the other items on the agenda'. COPAZ was to be made up of two representatives of the government (including one from the armed forces), two from the FMLN, and one from each of the parties or coalitions in the Legislative Assembly. It was to have the support of the UN Security Council — seen as a vital guarantee of its effectiveness — and the presence as observers of the Archbishop of San Salvador and a delegate of ONUSAL. The relatively strong representation of the opposition — in marked contrast to the Legislative Assembly — made COPAZ a model of the hoped for political reconciliation among Salvadoreans.

ONUSAL

Under the terms of the San José agreement of July 1990, the UN was to set up an observer mission, which came to be known as ONUSAL, to supervise the implementation of the Accords and to monitor human rights. The government subsequently agreed, however, to allow ONUSAL to arrive in the country in July 1991, before the signing of the Accords, with the limited mandate of human rights monitoring.

The presence of ONUSAL in the country at this early stage, as a brake on security force excesses, was crucial to the establishment of peace. With the signing of the Accords in January 1992, the mission expanded and took on its fuller mandate.

Implementation of the Accords

The ceasefire period declared from 1 February to 31 October 1992, by which date the government was to have implemented major structural and legislative reforms and the FMLN fully demobilised, was extremely short given the number of actions required by the Accords. In the end there were no major breaches of the ceasefire, though the deadlines invariably had to be extended as the government and FMLN used compliance as a bargaining counter.

The year was marked by a series of periods of heightened tension, caused by the failures to meet deadlines and differing interpretations of the agreements. Each side publicly logged the other's failures in fine detail but two issues dominated: the demobilisation of the armies and the land question. Throughout 1992 the discourse of both government and FMLN fluctuated between reconciliation and recrimination. At times death squad activity put the process in danger and extreme right propaganda reached fever pitch as the elite army battalions came up for dissolution. The intervention of the UN proved crucial on a number of occasions as the process appeared to reach deadlock; visits by the UN under-secretary, Marrack Goulding, were required to facilitate modifications to the timetable.

A key issue throughout 1992 was mutual compliance. The FMLN maintained that each side was bound to simultaneous fulfilment of commitments while the government claimed that each party to the Accords was separately committed and responsible directly to the UN secretary-general. This led to periods of paralysis as the FMLN halted its demobilisation until the government side caught up. It was only late in November that the UN openly accepted the FMLN interpretation after an extension of the ceasefire had been agreed.

The most dramatic immediate effect of the Accords was the new freedom of movement resulting from the ending of armed conflict and the return of the military to their barracks. This transformed the atmosphere both in the capital and in the rural areas, where for many years army permission was in reality, if not under law, required for travel. An impression, at least, of normality returned, and, without

CIIR Comment

FMLN sabotage of infrastructure, the way was opened for a revival of economic activity.

The timetable was adjusted twice in response to delays which brought the process to the brink of collapse, but the most acute crisis came in October. On 30 September, the FMLN announced the postponement of the third stage of its demobilisation, alleging that the government had failed to implement 64 points of the Accords, most importantly those dealing with the transfer of lands.

Military demobilisation

It was the military aspects of the Accords which at times seemed to put the whole process in jeopardy in 1992. In April, President Cristiani's good faith was called in question as he tried to avoid the dissolution of the National Guard and Treasury Police by merely changing their names to Military Police and Border Guards respectively. Although UN pressure led to the two security forces being disbanded as agreed, the manoeuvring was a sign of things to come.

Against a background of a right-wing propaganda campaign, ranging from paid advertisements demanding the maintenance of the Atlacatl battalion and rejecting an extension of the ceasefire to threats by the 'Maximiliano Hernández Martínez' death squads to assassinate FMLN leaders if the 31 October deadline for demobilisation was not met, on 21 October President Cristiani pulled out of negotiations to readjust the timetable. More worryingly, he also froze the dissolution of the Atlacatl battalion, which had carried out a massacre of peasants at Mozote in 1981 and the murders at the UCA in 1989. The FMLN put its forces on alert and warned of a planned army coup. Within a week, however, the government had agreed to a UN proposal to extend the timetable to 15 December and to reschedule the transfer of land.

For its part, the FMLN repeatedly delayed its gradual demobilisation, scheduled to take place in five stages. The first FMLN demobilisation, due on 1 May, was carried out two months late and it was not until 14 December, the eve of the extended ceasefire deadline, that the final 20 per cent of its forces were reintegrated into civilian life. The FMLN retained its surface-to-air missiles, however, promising to destroy them only after the purge of the armed forces had been carried out, according to the recommendations of the Ad Hoc Commission.

Despite the problems, by the first anniversary of the signing of the Peace Accords in January 1993, the FMLN had fully demobilised, the Treasury Police and National Guard had been dissolved and the government had demobilised 16 'anti-terrorist' battalions, including four of five elite forces, leaving only the Arce battalion still to be stood down.

The Ad Hoc and Truth commissions

Great tension surrounded the completion of the report of the Ad Hoc Commission into army human rights violations, which was submitted to the UN and President Cristiani on 23 September 1992. Although the findings were not published, reliable sources reported that over 100 officers were recommended for removal, including the entire high command. The President was committed to implementing the report by the end of November, but when the annual list of military appointments was announced on New Year's Eve, the measures fell far short of the commitments made to the UN secretary-general: no member of the high command was included in the changes.

One of the key moments in the implementation of the Peace Accords was the publication on 15 March 1993 of the report of the Truth Commission. The commission, set up under the Accords, consisted of Belisario Betancur, former president of Colombia, Reinaldo Figueredo Planchart, former Venezuelan foreign minister, and Thomas Buergenthal, professor of law at George Washington University. The commission received direct and indirect testimonies relating to over 23,000 victims. Because of limits of time and resources, the commission selected cases which were either particularly serious or typical of a general pattern. Among these were the killing of the Jesuits and two women in 1989, the massacres at El Mozote, Sumpul and El Calabozo, the 1980 murder of Archbishop Romero, and various acts of violence by the FMLN, including the murder of mayors.

The commission's findings fell most heavily on the various forces linked to the Salvadorean state: it attributed 85 per cent of human rights violations to agents of the state (including 60 per cent to the army) and 5 per cent to the FMLN.

The commission's recommendations, published, unlike the earlier report of the Ad Hoc Commission investigating the conduct of the army, called for the immediate dismissal of over 40 senior officers, including the minister of defence, General René Emilio Ponce, the vice-minister of defence, General Orlando Zepeda, held responsible for ordering the killings at the UCA, and almost the entire high command of the period. Those named were to be banned for ever from military or security duties, and for ten years from holding any public office in El Salvador. The commission declared 15 members of the FMLN guilty of human rights violations and recommended a ten-year ban on holding public office for ex-*comandantes* Joaquín Villalobos, Ana Guadalupe Martínez and Jorge Meléndez.

In addition the commission recommended measures to ensure civilian control of military promotions, the budget and all intelligence services, a legally backed provision allowing military personnel to disobey unlawful orders, measures to cut all ties between the military and private armed groups or other paramilitary groups, and 'the profound study of human rights' in all officer training courses.

The commission found the system of justice in El Salvador 'highly deficient' and recommended the immediate replacement of existing members of the Supreme Court, whose president, Dr Mauricio Gutiérrez Castro, it accused of 'unprofessional conduct'. It called for the reformed National Judicial Council provided for in the Peace Accords to be truly independent and for it, rather than the Supreme Court, to be responsible for appointing and dismissing judges. Among measures to guarantee the rights of accused, the commission proposed the banning of extra-judicial confessions, greater right of access to a lawyer, strict limits on pre-trial detention, and the publication of the whereabouts of all detention centres and the names of those detained.

Salvadorean government reaction to the report indicated the sensitivity of its findings. On the day before the report was officially released President Cristiani, in an address to the nation, called for mutual forgiveness and a 'general and absolute amnesty'. An amnesty bill was immediately submitted by the government to the Legislative Assembly, which passed it after five days' debate. The amnesty law covered all those involved in crimes during the war, except kidnapping, extortion and drug-trafficking.

Critics of the government argued that the law contravened the Inter-American Convention on Human Rights and probably the Salvadorean constitution as well. The Salvadorean non-governmental human rights commission unsuccessfully petitioned the Supreme Court to have the amnesty law declared unconstitutional. The US State Department criticised the amnesty as a guarantee of impunity, and Secretary of State Warren Christopher announced that the United States would seek to prosecute the officers named by the commission under international law. The US government suspended US$11 million of planned military aid and El Salvador's creditor banks, at their meeting in Paris, pressed the government for assurances that it would comply with the Truth Commission's recommendations. The European Community expressed concern at the amnesty law and called for the full implementation of the recommendations.

Once the amnesty law was passed, those principally affected launched a counter-offensive. Generals Ponce and Zepeda denounced the Truth Commission's report as 'totally biased and full of falsehood'. Ponce explained that it was part of an international conspiracy by 'the powers of the new world order' and 'a model for a plan to erase the concept of national sovereignty'. The nationalist card was played repeatedly in subsequent weeks by conservative politicians. The Supreme Court rejected the commission's report as 'damaging to the dignity of the country's justice system', and its members refused to resign.

Confusion reigned over the commission's recommendation that those named should be banned from holding office. On 4 April UN Secretary-General Boutros Boutros-Ghali accepted a Salvadorean government proposal that the 15 of the over 100 officers named by the Ad Hoc Commission in September 1992 who were still serving should leave their posts by 30 June 1993 and leave the army at the end of the year. The military ministers and the whole of the high command were replaced at the end of June, but the outgoing team received every sign of official approval, and specially voted generous pensions. The new team was described as very close to the views of their predecessors, and offering no guarantees of a thorough demilitarisation of Salvadorean society.

Human rights since the Accords
Despite the ending of general hostilities, abuses continued in many areas. Comparing the last five months of 1991 with the first five months of 1992, ONUSAL reported worrying increases in extra-judicial killings and death threats. It also noted that progress in creating institutional safeguards for human rights was very slow. It was not until April 1993 that the Legislative Assembly approved the names of the new independent National Judiciary Council, and even then some of the members were accused in the press of corruption and links with the military.

An early sign that death squads were still targeting opposition leaders was the murder on 2 March 1992 of trade unionist Nazario de Jesús Gracias. In August a leader of the FENASTRAS union federation, Ivan Ramírez, was murdered, and two days later a leader of the public works union was killed. Throughout the ceasefire period trade unionists, human rights workers and middle-ranking FMLN members were subject to attacks and death threats.

Throughout 1992 a nationwide crime wave created a general feeling of unease. Many cases of violent crime were reported to be the work of soldiers and members of the security forces, active or recently demobilised. Local human rights groups claimed that the government was tolerating political attacks under the cloak of common crime in an effort to curb the activities of the political opposition and the popular movement, and to continue the practice of impunity. The persistence of impunity was highlighted by an episode in April, when army major José Alfredo Jiménez fled unimpeded from jail, just five days after being condemned to 30 years' imprisonment for involvement in five kidnappings. In a less high profile case, in early October in Sensuntepeque, Cabañas, a witness who identified a military officer charged with fraud was found murdered the following day.

The exhumation of the victims of the El Mozote massacre, which began on 13 April 1992, under the auspices of the Truth Commission, illustrated how threatening to the government such human rights investigations were. By early November of that year the remains of some 199 bodies, mostly of old people and children, had been recovered and the team of specialist forensic scientists from Argentina reported that the evidence, including the absence of FMLN corpses, pointed to a massacre rather than a clash between army and guerrillas. This finding supported the charges of human rights groups that in December 1981 the US-trained Atlacatl battalion had killed some 1,000 peasants in this remote village in northern Morazán in what was probably the biggest massacre of the war.

The director of the government forensic science institute challenged the scientists' conclusion, claiming that the events at Mozote were 'massive violence during war time' and accused the Argentinians of politicising the investigation.

As investigation of human rights cases began, there was a wave of attacks on the media. The attacks included threats against journalists and an arson attack in July on the offices of the press agency,

SALPRESS, which destroyed its archives. The mainstream press continued its vitriolic attacks on the opposition, denouncing strikes and other protests as destabilisation by FMLN front organisations.

The activities of the human rights ombudsman were impeded by a lack of funds and his early reports were felt to underestimate the gravity of the continuing human rights abuses. By the end of April 1993, however, the ombudsman was expressing concern at the appearance of bodies with signs of torture, calling for a timetable for the implementation of the Truth Commission's recommendations and criticising the amnesty granted to those named by it as human rights violators.

The establishment of the new National Civilian Police has run consistently behind schedule; it was not until early August 1992, instead of May, as planned, that the first 660 students were taken on and by the end of the year only some 130 had graduated. Deployment of the first 500 graduates was rescheduled to February 1993. By mid-1993 it was estimated that in the crucial period in the run-up to the March 1994 elections, the new force would be deployed in only seven out of El Salvador's 14 departments. It is also reported that the new police force includes former members of the Treasury Police and National Guard, in violation of the Peace Accords. Meanwhile, ostensibly to meet the rising crime wave, in mid-1993 the government increased the strength of the National Police from 8,000 to 12,000, despite the provision of the Peace Accords that this force should be run down, arousing suspicions that ARENA wanted its own police force in action during the election campaign.

The sixth ONUSAL human rights report, published on 13 April 1993, criticised the ineffectiveness of the National Police and the judicial system. Echoing the findings of the Truth Commission, the report stated that the law reforming the National Judicial Council did not guarantee it sufficient independence and called for an immediate and total overhaul of all judicial bodies. Despite a continuing improvement in the human rights situation, the report stated that political murders were continuing and blamed ex-members of the armed forces and National Police. During the first three weeks of April alone 15 death squad-style murders were recorded. The director of the Tutela Legal human rights organisation commented: 'The death squads continue operating, using the same structures and methods.'

The slow pace of change in the whole area of law enforcement was illustrated on 20 May 1993, when riot police fired on a march by disabled veterans from both sides in the conflict, killing at least one person.

One issue which remained unresolved in mid-1993 was the large quantity of arms circulating in the country. This was illustrated in May 1993, when an explosion in Managua led to the discovery of five arms caches in Nicaragua belonging to the FPL faction of the FMLN. Subsequently another FMLN group, the ERP, handed over to the authorities an arms store hidden in San Salvador. These incidents — evidence of failure to comply with the Peace Accords — drew severe criticism from all quarters, including the UN secretary-general. The FMLN also confirmed reports of the existence of armed groups in northern Morazán and on the Guazapa volcano, but said that they were a mixture of former government and guerrilla troops dissatisfied with the slow pace of land distribution. While the existence of FMLN arms stores was given blanket media coverage, less attention was drawn to the fact that only 40 per cent of the arms reported by the army and the National Police to ONUSAL had been surrendered, and in addition unknown quantities of arms had been given by the security forces to civilians.

Land and reconstruction

Since the signing of the Accords, land issues have been a major focus of tension and conflict. The redistribution provisions in the Peace Accords were crucial to the resettlement of ex-combatants, and the regularisation of land occupations in the former conflict zones was vital for the security of the communities which had been established in those areas.

In July 1991, in the run-up to the peace agreements, the government had reached agreement with the main opposition peasant federation, the ADC, that in return for an end to land occupations, those who had occupied land before 3 July would be left undisturbed. The deal more or less held until the new year but the relative stability was broken as the Accords were signed.

The right wing claimed that massive land occupations were taking place, while the FMLN maintained that conflicts were actually arising from attempts by former owners to reclaim their properties without passing through the agreed procedures. It was only in late August 1992 that the COPAZ land sub-commission began to look at the FMLN inventory of 4,666 properties its supporters were claiming in the former conflict zones.

The lack of progress made by the end of September prompted the FMLN to postpone its scheduled demobilisation of the third 20 per cent of its forces. Although land disputes in the former conflict zones were to have been settled by the end of July 1992, as late as mid-October no FMLN ex-combatant had received a land title. By the end of the ceasefire period, 24 of 42 state farms had been transferred to FMLN ex-combatants but, while COPAZ had analysed some 2,200 of the private properties in the FMLN inventory, none had been handed over. Finance was a serious problem for redistribution, both for purchasing land to be redistributed and for providing the resources and credit essential to the new owners. At the end of 1992 it was estimated that US$97 million were still needed to finance the rest of the programme, which the UN was seeking from foreign donors.

In the context of the extension of the ceasefire period to mid-December 1992, the UN secretary-general proposed a new timetable for land distribution. Under the new proposal, approved by the Legislative Assembly just prior to the 15 December deadline, a total of 47,500 families would benefit, 7,500 ex-combatants of the FMLN, 15,000 ex-army troops and 25,000 land holders in the conflict zones. The distribution was rescheduled to take place in stages from January 1993, though as late as 1 May 1993 the director of ONUSAL reported that only 9,700 land grants had been made.

The National Reconstruction Programme (PRN) for the former conflict zones was heavily biased towards infrastructure, which took up 68 per cent of the budget, whereas social, health and education spending was allotted only 16 per cent, with 13 per cent destined to support for agriculture and industry. It was calculated that, over the five years of the programme, social spending for the 920,000 people who were to benefit would amount to no more than US$164 per head. By the end of 1992 implementation of the PRN was some way behind schedule.

Since the Peace Accords gave the government sole control over the implementation of the PRN, requiring it merely to consult the FMLN, fears have been expressed that it might use this significant inflow of international funds for its own political advantage. The bulk of the funds disbursed in the first year was channelled either through the 'Municipalities in Action' scheme created by the US Agency for International Development (USAID) — seen by many more as a counter-insurgency rather than development programme — or through non-governmental organisations (NGOs) close to the government. The local NGOs which had a record of working in these areas during the conflict were to a large extent marginalised. There have, however, been some more positive experiences of local cooperation and reconciliation, such as in Suchitoto where the ARENA mayor has welcomed popular participation in the process, despite coming under pressure from his own party, which removed him as local party secretary, and from USAID which threatened to block further aid unless opposition groups were excluded.

A more fundamental problem was revealed when freedom of movement was re-established after the ceasefire. The small production units established in communities such as Segundo Montes, in the former FMLN control zone of Morazán, making articles such clothes, footwear and furniture, were no longer able to compete when their closed markets were opened to competition from large manufacturers in the urban centres. This was an early example of the general problem facing small producers, who have figured as an important element in some alternative economic strategies for El Salvador.

The difficulties of formulating an economic policy agreed by all social groups in the country were illustrated by the problems of the Forum for Economic and Social Consensus (FES). The main employers' organisations boycotted the FES from May till September 1992, citing illegal takeovers of land as a threat to private property in general. Even then, the FES was dominated by conflicts over demands for trade union recognition in various companies which the employers opposed, with the support of the ministry of labour. The FES was brought into crisis by the refusal of the government and business leaders to ratify International Labour Organisation (ILO) conventions on trade union rights, arguing that they were unconstitutional.

The sixth ONUSAL human rights report, published in April 1993, noted that trade union activity in the country was being increasingly restricted. In the first half of 1993 there was increasing criticism that the country's political forces were not trying to make the FES work, preferring bilateral negotiations between the parties involved in disputes. The government itself also ignored the FES in formulating its economic measures, notably the value added tax introduced in September 1992.

The popular movement and the Accords

The problems of the FES highlight the challenges faced by what is known as the popular movement, a term which covers a wide range of groups including trade unions, organisations of peasants, women, the displaced, human rights organisations and other distinct social groups with social and economic demands. During the war years much of such activity was subordinated to the strategic aims of the FMLN, but with the end of hostilities various movements are redefining their own distinct objectives.

The most vigorous grassroots movement has been among peasants, around the issue of land reform. Occupations have taken place in defiance of the guidelines of the peasant organisations and of the FMLN. The Permanent Committee for the National Debate (CPDN) has developed out of its beginnings as a pressure group for peace negotiations and retains an important role. New women's organisations are forming with a more distinctively feminist agenda, partly as a result of the increasing importance of women as heads of households and community leaders during the war.

The trade union confederation UNTS has been active in organising protests against the refusal of government and employers to recognise trade union rights. Divisions among the teachers' trade unions were a problem in mid-1992, when the ANDES union declared a general strike while the federation to which it belonged was negotiating with the government. These divisions weakened the popular movement's capacity to respond to the government's economic package of September 1992, which introduced a value added tax and increased public service prices.

The most dramatic sign of divergences between the popular movement and the FMLN came in connection with the question of the purging of the armed forces. The willingness of some FMLN leaders to negotiate over the recommendations of the Ad Hoc and Truth commissions for sanctions against officers judged guilty of human rights abuses provoked outrage in many popular organisations, and was seen as a sign that the FMLN was unclear about what compromises were acceptable in the transition to peace and its own incorporation into institutional politics.

The economy and poverty

On taking office in June 1989, the ARENA government announced a Social and Economic Development Plan designed to create an efficient and diversified 'social market economy'. The first phase of the plan was a stabilisation programme designed to eliminate deficits in the trade balance and public finances, and to reduce inflation. Stabilisation was to have been achieved by December 1990, but the trade deficit increased by 40 per cent between 1991 and 1992, the public sector deficit doubled, and inflation, while falling slightly, was still, at 19 per cent per year, considerably above the government's target figure of 12 per cent. The country's balance of payments was only kept positive by an inflow of capital, consisting mainly of remittances from Salvadoreans in the United States and foreign aid for reconstruction.

The government's problems in achieving its objectives have been due partly to contradictions in its policies. The trade deficit, which the government has attributed to the fall in international coffee prices, has in fact been due mainly to an increase in imports following the government's reduction of tariffs as part of its trade liberalisation policy. This indicates that free trade, increasingly the cornerstone of the economic policies of all the Central American governments, is not a painless path to increased prosperity.

According to official figures, the gross domestic product (GDP) has grown steadily since 1989, from a rate of 1.1 per cent in 1991 to 4.6 per cent in 1992, though part at least of this increase must be attributed to the resumption of economic activity after the ending of hostilities. Government statistics also show a fall in unemployment and a decrease in poverty. But these figures are open to question, because the 10 per cent rise in real income in 1991-92 claimed by the government has to be set against a fall of 15 per cent in the period 1988-91 and a 50 per cent fall in real wages in the second half of the 1980s. The government's definition of poverty was also not sufficiently adjusted for inflation.

From 1989 to 1991, even according to traditionally cautious official figures, the numbers living in extreme poverty rose from 23.3 to 30 per cent, while those living below the poverty line rose from 55.3 to 64.1 per cent. Although GDP increased, the distribution of wealth worsened slightly during the same period. Despite the government's proclaimed desire to reduce poverty, in the period 1990-93 social spending has not increased as a proportion of total government spending and education and health spending even fell between 1991 and 1992, while service payments on the public debt were set to increase by 54 per cent. In addition, the government's measures to reduce the public sector deficit, notably the increase in public service charges and the introduction of value added tax, bore most heavily on the poor. According to official figures, unemployment overall fell between 1989 and 1992, from 8.3 per cent to 7.9 per cent, but urban unemployment increased from 7.5 per cent to 7.9 per cent. The greatest increases in the workforce were also in the age range 10-14, and among women, which may mean more mothers and children working to maintain the family income.

The policy which could do most in the medium term to raise the living standards of the population is the land distribution programme, provided that it is backed with adequate financial and technical assistance, and it is notable that this is an area where there have been most complaints of delay and inadequate resourcing.

Little progress has so far been made with the longer-term challenge of restructuring the economy towards alternative exports and creating employment in urban areas for the thousands of displaced who will not return to rural areas. Currently the country's economy is sustained by the remittances of Salvadoreans living in the United States and by reconstruction aid. This gives the government some scope for attacking the structural problems of the economy, but this inflow of capital will not continue indefinitely. The tasks of restructuring the economy and alleviating poverty will thus be urgent challenges for the government elected in 1994.

The moves towards free trade

In the long term, the prospects for El Salvador's economy and the welfare of its people depend on its relationship to the world economy. In view of the difficulties faced by small countries dependent on a small range of agricultural commodities such as coffee, the Salvadorean government, in common with the other governments of the region, sees the country's best chance in the process of regional integration, in order to create economies of scale and to give the Central American countries as a bloc more weight in international negotiations.

In May 1992 El Salvador joined Guatemala and Honduras (the 'northern triangle') in signing a free trade agreement which, in April 1993, with the accession of Nicaragua, became the Central American Free Trade Zone, replacing the Central American Common Market (CACM). The agreement reduced tariffs on intra-regional trade to a range of 5-20 per cent for some 5,000 products.

Before the agreement on the free trade zone, agreements had already been reached with Mexico, Colombia and Venezuela on moves towards setting up other multilateral free trade areas. In August 1992 Mexico signed an agreement known as the Multilateral

Liberalisation Accord with El Salvador, Guatemala, Costa Rica, Honduras and Nicaragua, which aimed for a free trade zone between the six countries by December 1996. Another agreement was signed in February 1993 between Colombia, Venezuela and the five Central American countries. This time the aim was to set up a free trade zone by 2003. As a first step, some duties were to be removed by July 1993.

The major impetus driving these moves has been the desire to link up with the North American Free Trade Agreement (NAFTA) formally signed by the presidents of Mexico, the United States and Canada in December 1992. The great hope of those in favour of free trade is that Central America will eventually have access to Mexican and US markets as part of an expanded NAFTA. But the free trade rush has given rise to several problems and doubts.

On the positive side, trade within Central America is expected to get a boost. Intra-regional trade was hit much harder as a result of the civil wars in the 1980s than trade with the United States and the rest of the world. In 1980 it had reached a peak of about US$1 billion, but had slumped to US$430 million by 1988. On the negative side, there are concerns about the structural limits to the expansion of intra-regional trade. Most of the Central American countries produce similar exports, both traditional goods (coffee, bananas, sugar, and cotton) and non-traditionals (garments and textiles). Regional trade, particularly exports, with Colombia and Venezuela is at a very low level at the moment and is unlikely to expand greatly.

In the case of El Salvador, given that the country has a more developed industrial base than the weaker and predominantly agricultural economies of Nicaragua and Honduras, integration may offer some benefits. But there are also likely to be major costs.

El Salvador, like the rest of Central America, is likely to suffer from the diverted trade and investment flows which many observers predict will affect many countries as a result of NAFTA. Analysts point out that Mexico will have a virtually unrivalled position in the region as a focus for investment, largely because of its much better access to US markets. Eventually, more Mexican goods will be exempt from tariffs than their Central American equivalents, which currently enjoy some advantages under the Caribbean Basin Initiative promoted by former President Reagan. Analysts claim Mexican textiles, and even sugar, for example, will have a decisive advantage.

And despite El Salvador's relative industrial competitiveness in Central America, there are signs that Mexico's less efficient industries, which will have difficulty competing in NAFTA, will try to treat the region as a captive market for their goods. The further economic restructuring required to meet the free trade challenge could exacerbate social conflict in El Salvador at a time when the consolidation of peace is an urgent need.

Political forces and the 1994 elections

Unquestionably the most important development in Salvadorean politics since 1989 has been the shift of the social conflict from the military to the political sphere. The chief symbol of this transformation is the public presence in the country of the FMLN as a recognised political participant, sealed on 14 December 1992 by its formal recognition as a legitimate political party.

While obviously bringing advantages, this transformation has confronted the FMLN with formidable challenges. The most elementary was the complexity of the demands upon it: at the same time as it had to carry out the demobilisation of its forces and keep constantly alert for the attempts of the armed forces to evade their obligations, it had to organise itself throughout the country as a political movement and take its place alongside the other political actors. And now, as a political organisation, it has to find funds and adequate media outlets, and adapt the habits of an underground military organisation to those of public political life. The unity achieved by the military command during the war has not been maintained since the Accords, as the five groups making up the FMLN have tended to reassert their individual identities.

At the other end of the political spectrum, ARENA, as the party in government during the negotiations, is in a strong position. President Cristiani and his party have now been recognised by the FMLN as legitimate, and in domestic political terms the party enjoys the advantage of being in power and in control of reconstruction funds, a situation its efficient electoral machine will use to its advantage in the run-up to 1994. The business sector is likely to see ARENA as the best protector of its interests in the immediate future, but whether this means the continued development of ARENA into a more pragmatic party has been cast in doubt by the selection of the hardline mayor of San Salvador, Armando Calderón Sol, as the party's presidential candidate, reflecting the strength within the party base of groups hostile to the concessions required by the Peace Accords.

ARENA has also benefited from the decline of the Christian Democrats, as the result of the PDC's inefficiency and corruption in government under President Duarte from 1984 to 1989. A right-wing faction of the PDC broke away to form the Authentic Christian Movement (MAC) and join the ARENA-led coalition in the Legislative Assembly.

The entry of the FMLN into constitutional politics has squeezed the other parties of the left and centre-left. The Democratic Convergence (CD), a coalition formed in 1988 from the Popular Social Christian Movement (MPSC), the Social Democratic Party (PSD), the Revolutionary National Movement (MNR) and more recently joined by the Nationalist Democratic Union (UDN), has been weakened by the withdrawal of the MNR. Both the MPSC and the MNR have the advantage of having taken part in constitutional politics since the return of their leaders from exile in late 1987. As the CD, they gained eight seats in the 1991 Legislative Assembly elections and have established themselves as parliamentary actors. The death of the MNR's two best known leaders, Guillermo Ungo and Hector Oquelí, has left Rubén Zamora of the MPSC, currently vice-president of the Legislative Assembly, as the outstanding centre-left political figure.

With the completion of the demobilisation, short-term political considerations are dominated by the general elections due in 1994, when all offices in the political system have to be filled, president, vice-president, deputies and mayors of municipalities.

According to surveys carried out by the UCA's polling institute, in the year following the signing of the Peace Accords ARENA remained the party with the greatest declared support, with the FMLN in second place. All the surveys in this period showed almost 50 per cent of those interviewed expressing no preference, perhaps an indication of continuing fear to express political opinions, as well as a considerable degree of uncertainty. The FMLN was given a boost in the January and February 1992 celebrations to mark the signing and implementation of the Peace Accords, its events attracting far higher numbers than those organised by the government and ARENA. In February 1993 support for the three main parties was: ARENA 16.9 per cent, the FMLN 7.3 per cent and the PDC 6.9 per cent. The proportion of voters indicating 'no preference' remained high at 48 per cent.

In the period up to the 1994 elections, three factors will be crucial: the security situation for political campaigning, the state of the electoral register and the ability of the opposition to create a credible alternative to ARENA.

The electoral registration campaign carried out in early 1993 is said to have reached only one-third of its target of registrations. With five months left to register voters, the Supreme Electoral Tribunal reported that almost 700,000 of the 2.7 million Salvadoreans eligible to vote did not have voter registration cards, 194,000 of them in San Salvador.

The choice of a combined opposition presidential ticket to oppose ARENA's Calderón Sol is proving highly complex, and may not be resolved before the second round of voting in 1994. Rubén Zamora was adopted as candidate by the CD in May 1993 and the largest group within the FMLN, the Popular Liberation Forces (FPL), backed a ticket combining Zamora as presidential candidate and the FPL's Facundo Guardado as vice-presidential candidate. Other groups within the FMLN argued that the Zamora-Guardado ticket was too left-wing and that the party should support a centrist ticket, including the Christian Democrats. But this possibility was weakened when the PDC chose as its candidate Fidel Chávez Mena, associated with the discredited Christian Democrat policies of the early 1980s. The CD-FPL alliance was also cast in doubt after the discovery of FPL arms caches in June 1993.

The church

Historically the church in El Salvador, as in Latin America as a whole, has been allied with the wealthy landowners and the rich industrial and commercial sectors of society: with these elites, and the all-powerful military, it has been seen and has seen itself as one of the pillars of the state.

This privileged position began to be eroded when the bishops of the continent, meeting at Medellín, Colombia, in 1968, declared that the church's mission committed it to work for social justice. The now-famous 'preferential option for the poor', proclaimed at the subsequent meeting in Puebla, Mexico, in 1979 and reaffirmed in Santo Domingo, the Dominican Republic, in October 1992, became the basis for a new model of church, built on small base communities, expressing and exploring their faith in a situation of injustice and joining in the struggle for a more just and humane social and economic system. Base communities in El Salvador, in all the churches, were to a large extent the backbone of the struggle for social justice, many joining the guerrilla army when peaceful avenues were closed.

The Salvadorean hierarchy was not ready for this radical analysis and shift, and to this day is divided between a minority faithful to the spirit of Medellín and Puebla and those upholding conservative principles and the status quo.

Romero and the option for the poor

The conservatives welcomed the appointment in 1977 of Oscar Arnulfo Romero as Archbishop of San Salvador, confident that this somewhat timid man, nervous of the smallest departure from traditional ways (and especially nervous of so-called political priests), would not disturb the established order. Romero's timidity, however, gave way to his strength when he was confronted with the scale of social injustice and violence in El Salvador. The murder of his friend, the Jesuit Rutilio Grande, was a turning point and he became increasingly outspoken. His Sunday homilies, which were broadcast, became national events, denouncing the latest atrocities and offering a Christian commentary on Salvadorean life. In his pastoral letters he developed a theology which accompanied the popular movements, fiercely defending their right to organise to build a just society, though always critical of wanton violence.

Romero became in his lifetime the patron saint of those sectors of the church, in El Salvador as elsewhere in Latin America, which remained faithful to the option for the poor, and for that reason became the targets of the conservative right wing of church and state. His position was confirmed on 24 March 1980, when he was murdered by a death squad.

Mgr Arturo Rivera Damas, Romero's only ally among the bishops, was appointed apostolic administrator of the Archdiocese of San Salvador on Romero's death, and three years later was himself appointed Archbishop.

The repression continued through the 1980s. The legal aid service of the Archdiocese, Tutela Legal, which was started by the Jesuits in 1975 as Socorro Jurídico, and at Archbishop Romero's request was made an official organisation of the Archdiocese, carried out courageous and painstaking work throughout this period, compiling dossiers of human rights violations and identifying the victims of the brutal murders.

The decade that had begun with the murder of Archbishop Romero ended in November 1989 with the massacre at the UCA of six Jesuit priests and two women workers. The Jesuits were regarded by the army high command as 'subversives', rightly in the sense that, under the leadership of Ignacio Ellacuría, they had made the UCA the centre of a powerful critique of the economic and social system prevailing in El Salvador. At the same time, they proved a powerful and influential advocate, even among the elites, of peace and reconciliation based on social justice. The UCA is also the base of Jon Sobrino, one of Latin America's leading theologians.

The struggle for peace and justice

The Catholic Church has not been alone in its support for the poor and the powerless during these years. Christians of other churches have worked side by side with Catholics and the leaders of the Lutheran and Episcopalian churches have suffered persecution for their principled stand on behalf of the victims of injustice. All churches united in a National Debate for Peace, which the Jesuits of the UCA had a share in organising, and which was sponsored by the Archdiocese of San Salvador. Archbishop Rivera had acted as an intermediary between both sides in the civil war. Throughout the peace negotiations the National Debate for Peace was vigorous and vocal in its insistence that the agenda of the poor be heard, and that a new just and democratic society be built on the ruins of the war.

A problem for the churches which the peace process has left intact is that of the small pentecostal churches which have been proliferating in El Salvador, as in the rest of Latin America. With their livelier worship and more flexible organisation, they are drawing large numbers of Christians away from all the historic churches, both Catholic and Protestant. They are often criticised for withdrawing people from the struggle for a more just society, and confining them to a personal, inward-looking religion. In some cases this has been a deliberate tactic, financially backed by conservative North American Christians, but the deeper challenge to the historic churches is a religious one, and one they have not yet found a way of meeting. The Catholic Church has been hampered in this by Vatican disapproval of base communities, which might otherwise have provided a richer model of church life rooted in popular culture.

The role of the international community

The El Salvador peace process has been seen by some as a model for international action under the so-called 'new world order'. The role of the UN, first under Javier Pérez de Cuéllar and subsequently under

Boutros Boutros-Ghali, has been crucial, and the role of its observer mission, ONUSAL, has been an important precedent.

The UN could not have played such a forceful role without the backing of the Security Council, and principally of the United States, but the degree to which the principles underlying US policy have changed is open to question.

The Clinton administration's first policy statement on Latin America, made by Deputy Secretary of State Clifton Wharton on 3 May 1993, contains a commitment to human rights, but the underlying message is the association of 'open markets and democratic values'. This reflects the 1991 shift in strategy of the USAID programme from development based on counter-insurgency to export-led growth based on the private sector. In this approach US assistance has been directed towards the reduction of the state sector and the promotion of large-scale business, to the exclusion of medium and small producers. If this approach continues, the social inequalities which originally provoked the conflict in El Salvador, and which still remain, will be reinforced.

Other countries have given close support to the peace process, notably Mexico, Venezuela, Colombia and Spain, the 'friends of the secretary-general'. Spain is offering financial assistance for the training of the new civilian police force.

The European Community (EC) defined its relationship to Central America in the 1984 San José agreement, one of the key elements of which is support for democracy. EC financial support for refugees returning from exile in the late 1980s was crucial to their successful resettlement. Perhaps more importantly, this aid, which was destined primarily for areas under FMLN influence, was a strong diplomatic signal of European disapproval of government military actions there and of the US financing of the Salvadorean armed forces. This support was crucial also in assisting the development of local non-governmental groups through which the aid was channelled and the development of alternative rural development experiments. A welcome sign that the promotion of democracy in Central America remains one of the principles of EC policy was its call at the San José meeting in March 1993 for the full implementation of the Truth Commission's recommendations.

The successful conclusion of the peace process requires financial and technical support for land redistribution and resettlement programmes, and for the strengthening of new institutions such as the civil police, the office of the human rights ombudsman and the National Judicial Council.

The role of foreign aid here will be crucial. In addition to economic assistance, diplomatic contact will remain vital during the further stages of the peace process, as was shown by the crucial role played by UN intervention during the various crises of the demobilisation process.

Future prospects

The Salvadorean Peace Accords were hailed by both UN Secretary-General Boutros Boutros-Ghali and the FMLN as ushering in a 'negotiated revolution', but the evidence of the 18 months since the signature of the Accords is that El Salvador's deep economic and social divisions will not be easily bridged. While war-weariness and the removal of superpower rivalry may reduce the likelihood of a resumption of large-scale armed conflict, transformation of the judiciary, of land distribution and of economic relations in general are not precisely outlined in the Accords, nor is there any effective mechanism for keeping the parties in dialogue. The difficulties of the Economic and Social Forum highlight this problem.

The crises in the implementation of the Accords to date have been overcome only by the intervention of the UN, but ONUSAL is due to leave after the 1994 elections, after which international interest may be expected to decline. In any event, international pressure alone cannot resolve Salvadorean conflicts.

A key weakness of the Accords is that they were negotiated between only two Salvadorean parties, the government and the FMLN, with the acquiescence of the armed forces, and there is a tendency for disputes to be settled by bilateral negotiation between these two, to the exclusion of other actors in Salvadorean society, other political parties, trade unions and community organisations, and business leaders. International support for the peace process in El Salvador must now be directed primarily towards encouraging whole-hearted acceptance of the compromise by Salvadoreans themselves. The concept of reconciliation based on justice, so dear to Ignacio Ellacuría, is very important here, and this is not just a matter of moral suasion, but also involves education and the strengthening of the organisations of civil society so that all Salvadoreans can have a say in their future. Judicious use, or witholding, of development aid will be vital in this.

The period between now and the 1994 elections is crucial. If a reforming coalition is elected, there is good hope that El Salvador can continue in peace to face the immense challenges of reconstruction. If an ARENA government emerges with new legitimacy from UN-sponsored elections, there is no such guarantee. The peace process is not yet irreversible.

The other contribution the international community can make to peace in El Salvador is progress towards the construction of a fairer international financial and trading system in which small countries are able to participate in the global economy. The models so far on offer leave much to be desired in this respect. Here there is a continuing role for the international solidarity called forth by the courage and self-sacrifice of so many Salvadoreans in the last 20 years. For the sake of humanity, as well as for El Salvador, their vision must be kept alive.

Further reading

Barry, T., *El Salvador: A Country Guide*, Albuquerque, New Mexico: Inter-Hemispheric Education Resources Center, 1991, available in Britain from the Latin American Bureau.

Brockman, J.R., *Romero, Bishop and Martyr*, London, 1982; US ed. *The Word Remains: A Life of Oscar Romero*, Maryknoll, NY, 1982.

CIIR, *Romero, Martyr for Liberation*, London 1982.

— *Central America: Braving the New World*, London 1992.

Dunkerley, J., *Power in the Isthmus*, London and New York: Verso, 1988.

Galdámez, P., *Faith of a People: The Life of a Basic Christian Community in El Salvador*, Maryknoll, NY, London and Victoria, 1986.

Hussey, P., *Free From Fear: Women in El Salvador's Church*, London 1989.

Pearce, J., *Promised Land: Peasant Rebellion in Chalatenango, El Salvador*, London: Latin America Bureau, 1986.

— *Under the Eagle: US Intervention in Central America and the Caribbean*, London, 2nd ed., Latin America Bureau, 1982.

Sundaram, A., and Gelber, G. (ed.), *A Decade of War: El Salvador Confronts the Future*, London 1991.

Vigil, M.L., *Death and Life in Morazán*, London 1989.

Wright, S., *El Salvador: A Spring Whose Waters Never Run Dry*, Washington DC and London, 1990.